LITERACY LINE-UP

NON FICTION

WRITTEN AND COMPILED BY
DAVID ORME

CONTENTS

Report on Planet 4

Mars is much further from the Sun than the Earth, and is much smaller. It is a cold, dry planet with a thin atmosphere. It has two tiny moons called Phobos and Deimos.

A photograph of Mars taken by the Viking orbiter.

Is there life on Mars?

There is no water on the surface of Mars, and the atmosphere is too thin to breathe, so life there is unlikely. However, there are signs that there was once water on the planet, so there may have been life on Mars millions of years ago. Some scientists believe that there may still be life deep down under the surface.

The Viking lander sampled dust from these sand dunes to test for traces of life on Mars.

A rocky, dusty world

Mars is a rocky, dusty world, with deep canyons and huge, dead volcanoes. The volcano Olympus Mons is three times higher than Mount Everest. Vast dust storms often sweep across the planet.

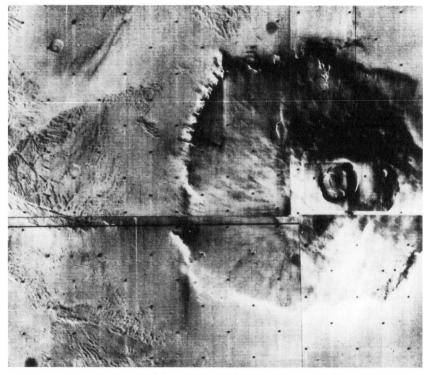

The Olympus Mons, a huge volcano on Mars, far higher than any mountain on earth.

Exploring Mars

Many unmanned probes have been sent to Mars. Some have simply flown past, taking photographs, while others have landed and carried out experiments on the rocks and soil. In the next century there may be a manned mission to Mars. This will be very difficult as the return trip will take a number of years.

Viking Lander 1, which investigated the soil on Mars and took the first photographs of a new world.

Mars and Earth compared

Mars is 228 million kilometres from the Sun, while the Earth is 150 million kilometres away. Its diameter is 6,794 kilometres, compared with the 13,756 of the Earth. The average temperature on the surface is -23° Celsius, 50 degrees lower than the Earth. A day on Mars is almost the same length as an Earth day, but a year is nearly twice as long.

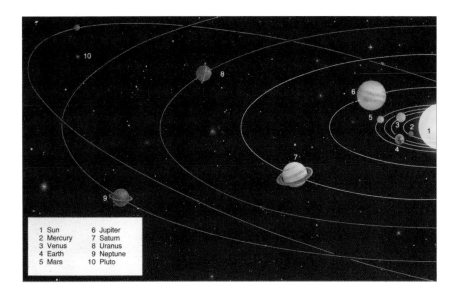

1 Sun	6 Jupiter
2 Mercury	7 Saturn
3 Venus	8 Uranus
4 Earth	9 Neptune
5 Mars	10 Pluto

AN EXPLANATION
How does a mobile phone work?

Mobile phones have become very popular these days. Whether you are out walking, in your car or on a train, you can always be in touch. But how do mobile phones actually work?

1 The phone itself

A mobile phone handset is a powerful radio transmitter and receiver.
It consists of a complex electronic package attached to a rechargeable battery.

Mobile phone

A mobile phone communicates by radio with its nearest base station aerial. This message is relayed to a mobile telephone network exchange, which then connects the call to the public switched telephone network (PSTN). This is the network to which all fixed telephones are also linked.

Base station

PSTN

Mobile phone exchange

A keypad enables the user to key in the number being called, and carry out various other functions. It is possible to access a memory, change the ringing tone, or even send a text message or go on line to the Internet. A small display screen shows information such as the signal strength and how much charge is left in the battery.

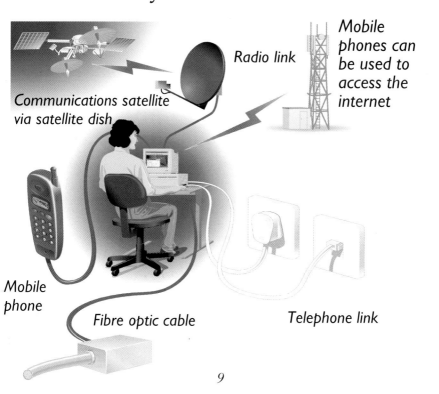

Communications satellite via satellite dish

Radio link

Mobile phones can be used to access the internet

Mobile phone

Fibre optic cable

Telephone link

Making a call involves:

1 keying in the number of the person being called,

2 pressing 'send',

3 pressing 'end call' when the call is over.

When the phone rings, the 'receive call' button is pressed so that the incoming call can be heard.

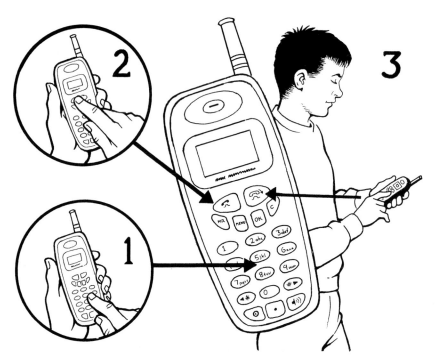

2   The mobile phone network

Mobile phones are more correctly called 'cellular' phones. The country is divided into many small areas or cells, each with its own transmitter and receiver.

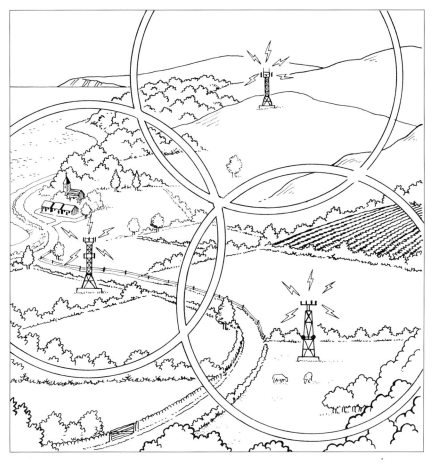

When you switch on your phone, it sends out an identification signal which is picked up by the nearest receiver, then sent by a cable to the telephone call centre. Here a computer will record the location of the phone. If you are on the move, and enter a new 'cell', your phone will send another signal and the computer will update its records.

In this way, if someone dials your mobile number the call centre will always know where you are, and can connect you to your caller. If your phone is switched off, or you are in an area with no signal such as down in a valley, the call centre will take a message for you. When you switch on your phone, or when the phone reconnects with the call centre, you will be able to hear your message.

Travelling to school

At the start of the school day the road outside any school is choked with cars as children are dropped off at school. This causes congestion and may even lead to accidents. Many people feel that walking to school is a much better option, but not everyone agrees!

Legs are best!

Supporters of walking to school claim that car travel is not only bad for the environment, but bad for the travellers too.

Travelling to school by car means that:

• The roads have extra congestion during particularly busy times, such as the morning rush hour.

- The cars add to air pollution. Often the journey to school is only a short one, and the first few miles of a car's journey are the most polluting as the engine is not yet warm enough to be really efficient.

- The great numbers of cars outside the school in the morning and afternoon cause problems for others. Often there is nowhere to park, and cars block the road. Parked cars make it difficult for children walking to school to cross the road in safety.

- Local residents become annoyed as parents' cars often block their driveways.

- Higher petrol prices makes car journeys increasingly expensive. After all, walking is free – all it needs is for parents and children to leave home a little earlier!

I love my car!

The arguments in favour of walking sound good, but life isn't that simple! Parents will bring children to school because:

• They feel it is safer that way. Often parents cannot walk children to school – they may have more than one child at different schools.

• A walking journey to school that involves crossing roads can be dangerous, especially in the winter when it is dark.

• Walking may be fine when the weather is good, but not when it is pouring with rain.

• Sometimes children live a long way from school, and walking isn't an option.

• Some parents drop children off at school on the way to work. It would not be very sensible to walk to school with them, then walk home again to collect the car.

• Children often have to carry heavy belongings to and from school – books, lunch boxes, P.E. kit and equipment, even musical instruments.

Making the right choice

Convenience versus the environment – this is the choice we all have to make. The answer is compromise – don't use your car just to be lazy, walk whenever you can; and if you can't, why not share a car journey with someone else? If everyone shared a journey with a friend, there would only be half the number of cars – and think how much better that would be!

How to make a garden for a person with a visual handicap

*E*ven though visually handicapped people's sight may be poor, or they may even have no sight at all, they can enjoy gardens. There is much more to a garden than simply looking at flowers.

1 Making the garden safe

People with a visual handicap need a safe environment in which to enjoy the garden. Make footpaths wide and even, if possible without steps. Bushes are better than walls at the edge of paths, but don't use holly or other prickly plants. Handrails can be useful to guide people round the garden.

2 Appealing to the senses

Sound   There are many ways to bring attractive sounds into the garden. Hang wind chimes, and look for plants such as trees and grasses that will rustle when the wind blows.

Two very important sources of sound are

a running water and

b birds

so if possible install a water feature and plant flowers and shrubs that provide food for birds – and don't forget the bees!

Smell Choose plants that have interesting and attractive scents, and aromatic herbs that can be rubbed in the hands such as lavender and rosemary.

Feel Think about different textures that can give an interesting feel to the garden – these can be the leaves and stems of plants, the bark of trees, or even a range of rough and smooth stones. Don't forget, too, to vary the texture of the path by using different types of gravel and flagstones. This will be a useful guide for people with a visual handicap as they will soon learn where they are in the garden from the feel and sound of the path beneath their feet.

Finally, don't forget the sense of taste. Everyone enjoys the flavour of fresh fruit and vegetables from the garden!

A recipe for kedgeree

Kedgeree is based on a traditional Indian dish.

Ingredients:

*500 grammes of smoked fish
   such as haddock*
250 grammes of long grain rice
2 eggs
100 grammes of butter
Chopped parsley
Cayenne pepper if liked
Seasoning

Method:

1 Boil the rice until nearly cooked. At the same time poach the fish in a frying pan with enough water to cover it for 10–15 minutes, or until tender.

2 Boil the eggs until they are hard. Shell them, then chop one into small pieces and slice the other into rounds.

3 Melt the butter in a frying pan. Add all the ingredients except the parsley and stir over a moderate heat until hot.

4 Garnish with the parsley before serving.

Serves four

27

Thesaurus

A thesaurus lists synonyms (words or phrases of similar meaning).

Rush   run, dash, race, hurry, sprint, speed, scurry, scamper, scuttle, gallop, canter, charge, full tilt, full pelt, belt (*slang*), get your skates on (*slang*), go hell for leather (*slang*), break the speed limit, step on the gas (*slang*)

Dictionary

A dictionary gives definitions (meanings) of words. Sometimes a dictionary gives other information such as the origin of the word and how to pronounce it.

Rush

1 *(noun)* *Old English* A plant with tall stalk-like leaves growing in marshy ground or along the banks of rivers.

2 *(noun)* A sudden, fast movement.

Rush-hour: the time of day when traffic is busiest.

(verb) To move with great speed, to hurry.

3 *(noun)* The first print of a film before editing.

4 *(noun)* Old name for a disease in cattle.

Glossary

A glossary defines unusual or technical words and phrases.

Report on planet 4

atmosphere the gasses surrounding a planet.

canyon deep rocky valley

Celsius temperature scale in which 0° represents the freezing point of water.

diameter length of a straight line through the centre of a sphere or circle.

dust storm a strong wind carrying dust.

probe a spacecraft designed to send back information.

unmanned without people.

volcano mountain with openings through which molten rock and gasses are, or have been released.

How does a mobile phone work?

handset piece of equipment designed to be held in the hand.

Internet the world-wide information and communication system based on computers

keypad part of a telephone with push-buttons.

receiver equipment for receiving radio messages.

rechargeable describes a battery that can be re-used.

text message message that is written, not spoken.

transmitter equipment for sending radio messages.

Travelling to school

congestion road hold-ups caused by too much traffic.

environment the surroundings in which people, plants and animals live.

pollution unwanted and possibly harmful materials in the environment.

rush hour the time of day when traffic is busiest.

Making a garden

aromatic strongly scented.

flagstones square or rectangular flat stones used to make paths.

textures the feel of different surfaces.

visually handicapped having serious difficulties with sight.

water feature a garden item involving water, such as a pond or a fountain.

wind chimes pieces of metal or other material that make musical sounds when blown together by the wind.